Contents

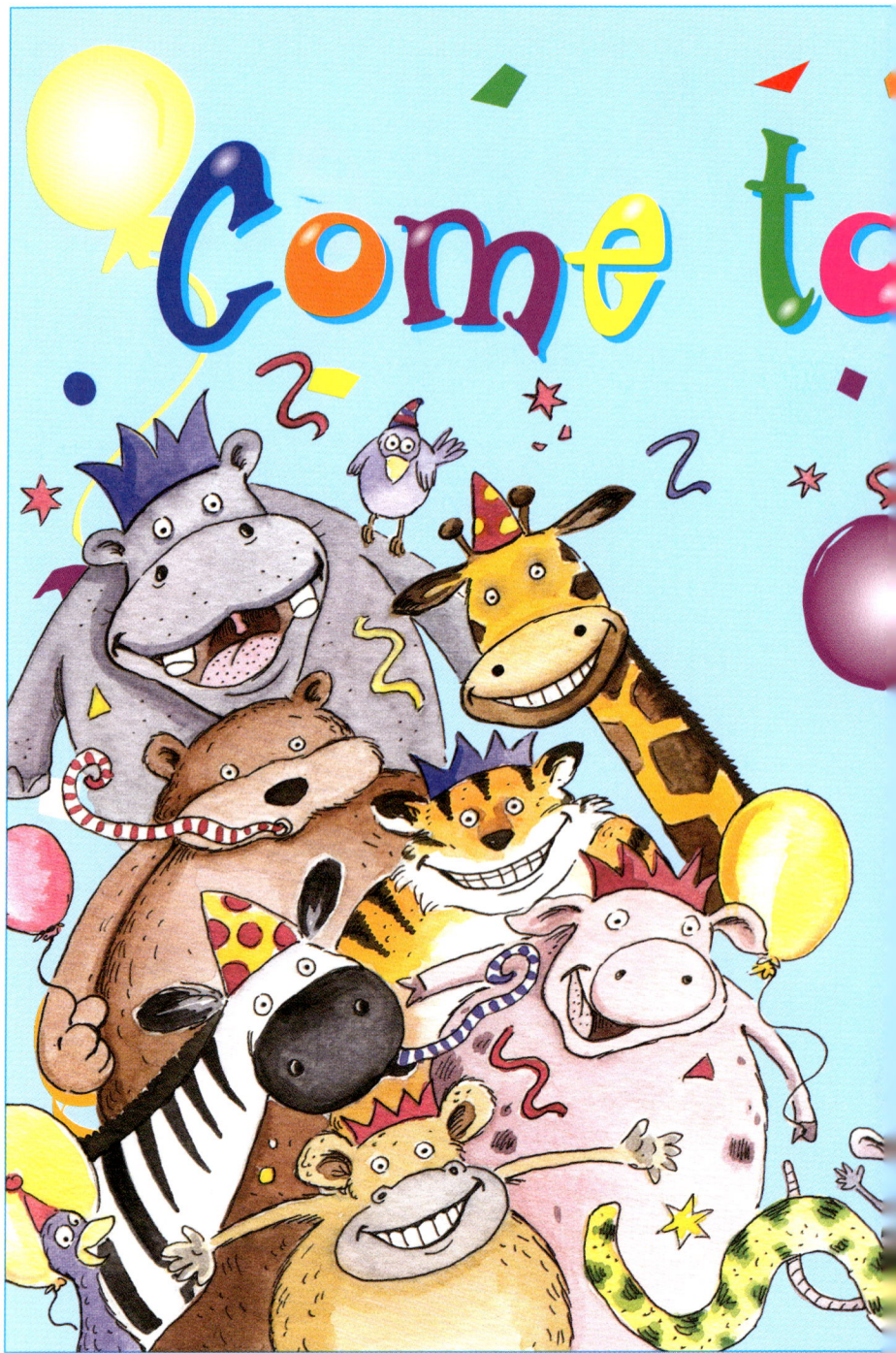

2

my party

An invitation

From: Janet

Place: At my house

Date: After school on Friday

Time: At four o'clock

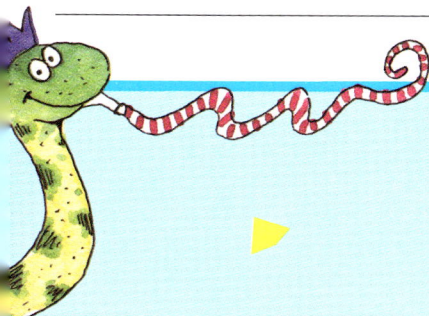

Find my house on the map.

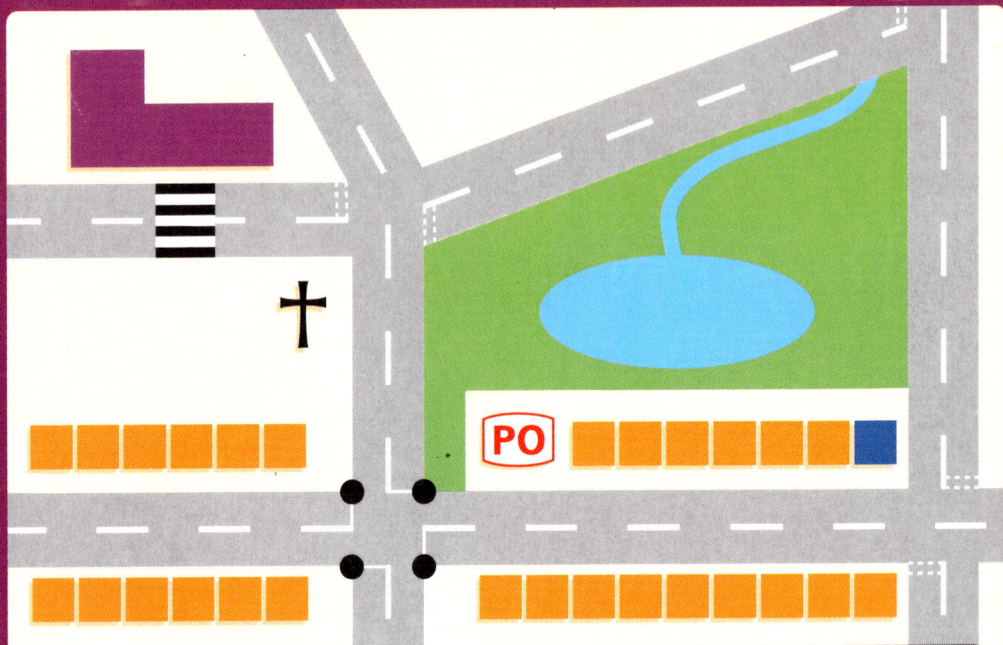

Key

School	
Zebra crossing	
Church	
Traffic lights	

PO	Post office
	House
	My House
	Grass
	Pond

4

5

First cross at the zebra crossing.

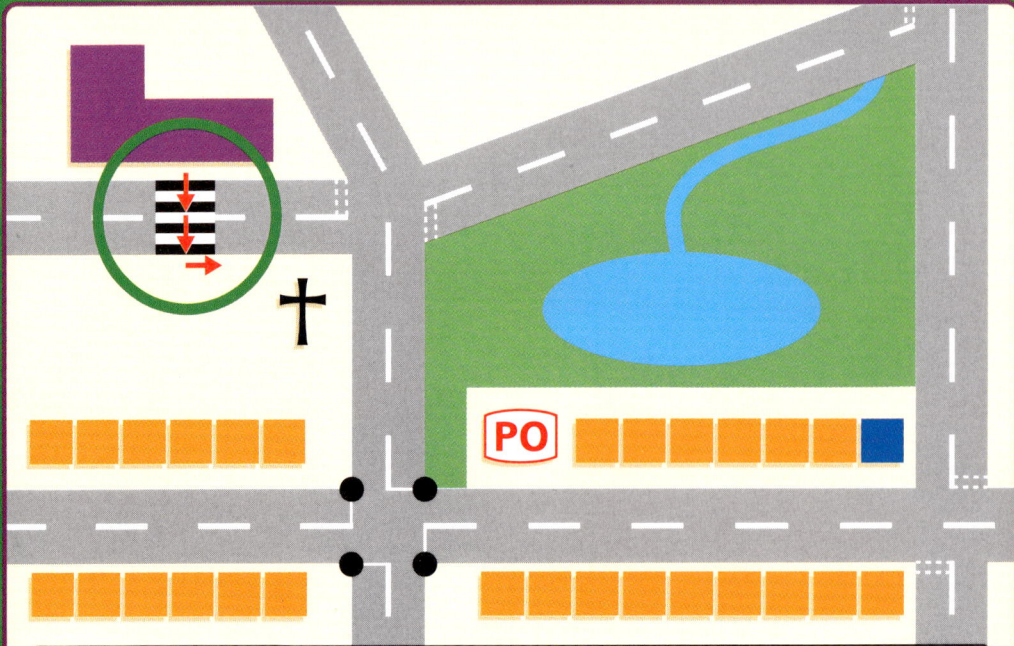

PO

Key

School		**PO**	Post office
Zebra crossing			House
Church			My House
Traffic lights			Grass
			Pond

Turn right past the church.

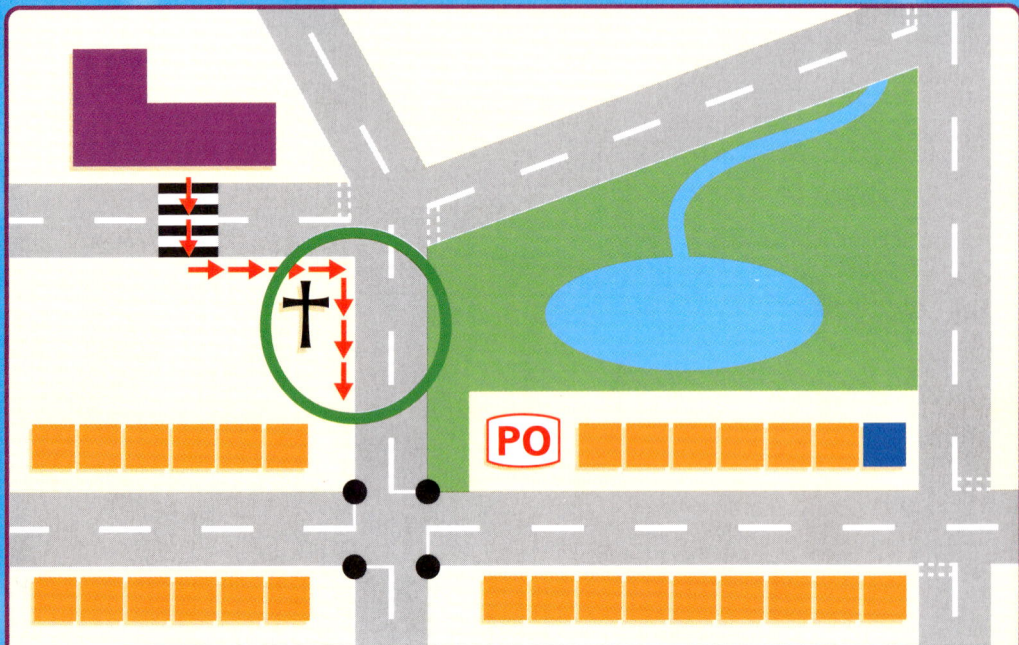

Key

School		PO	Post office
Zebra crossing			House
Church			My House
Traffic lights			Grass
			Pond

Patrol

9

Then carry on until you get to the traffic lights.

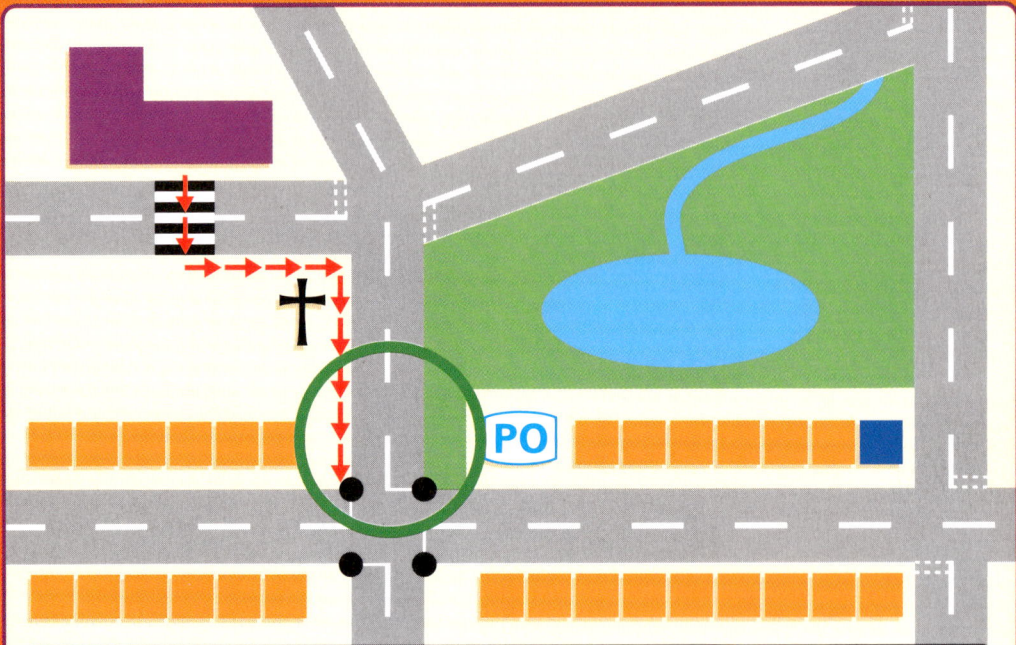

Key

School		PO	Post office
Zebra crossing			House
Church			My House
			Grass
Traffic lights			Pond

11

Now turn left and when the green man is showing, cross the road.

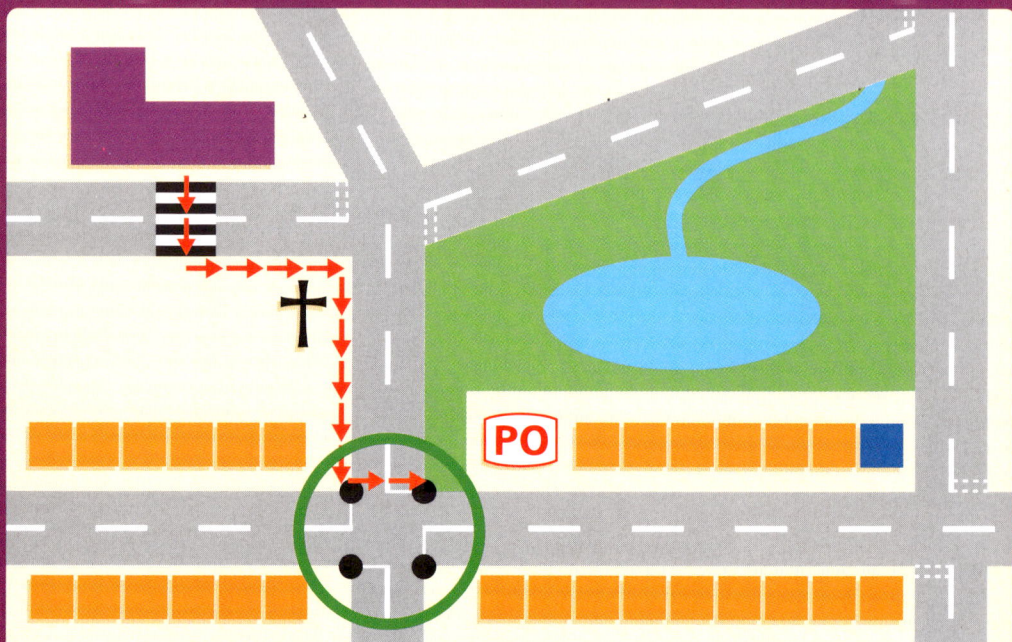

Key

School		PO	Post office
Zebra crossing			House
Church			My House
Traffic lights			Grass
			Pond

13

Walk past the park and look out for the post office.

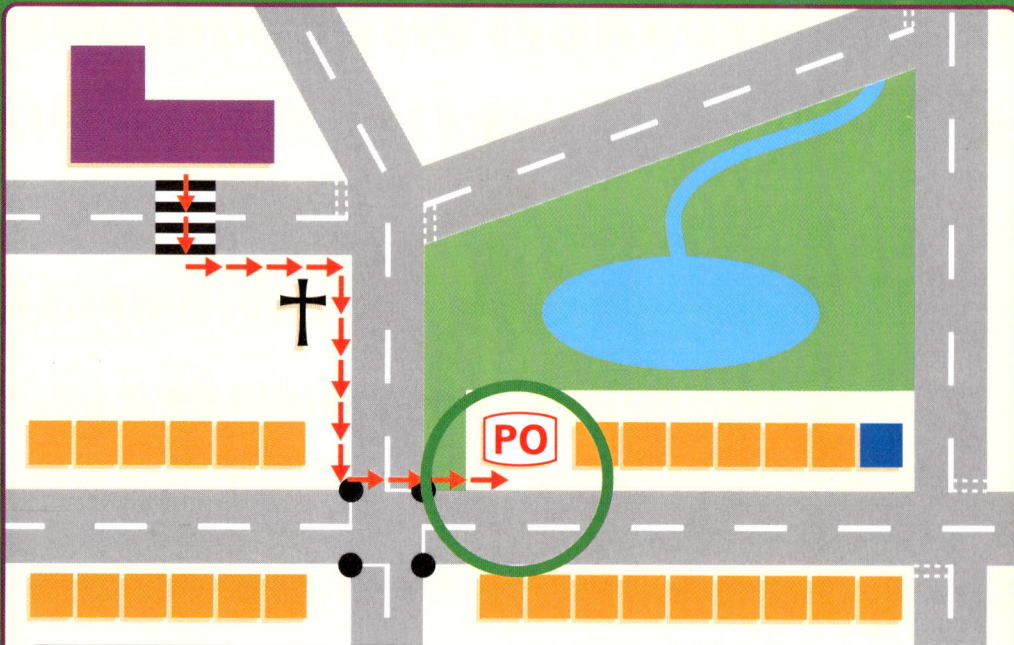

Key

School	
Zebra crossing	
Church	
Traffic lights	

PO	Post office
	House
	My House
	Grass
	Pond

Count six houses after the post office.

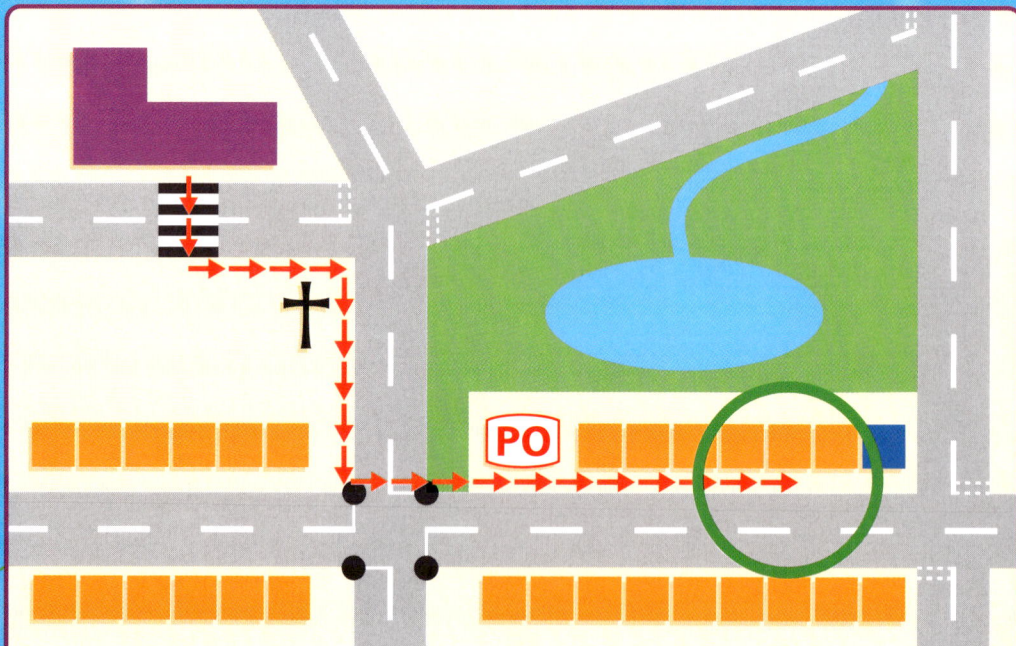

Key

	School	**PO**	Post office
	Zebra crossing		House
	Church		My House
	Traffic lights		Grass
			Pond

Look for the blue door with the balloons on it.

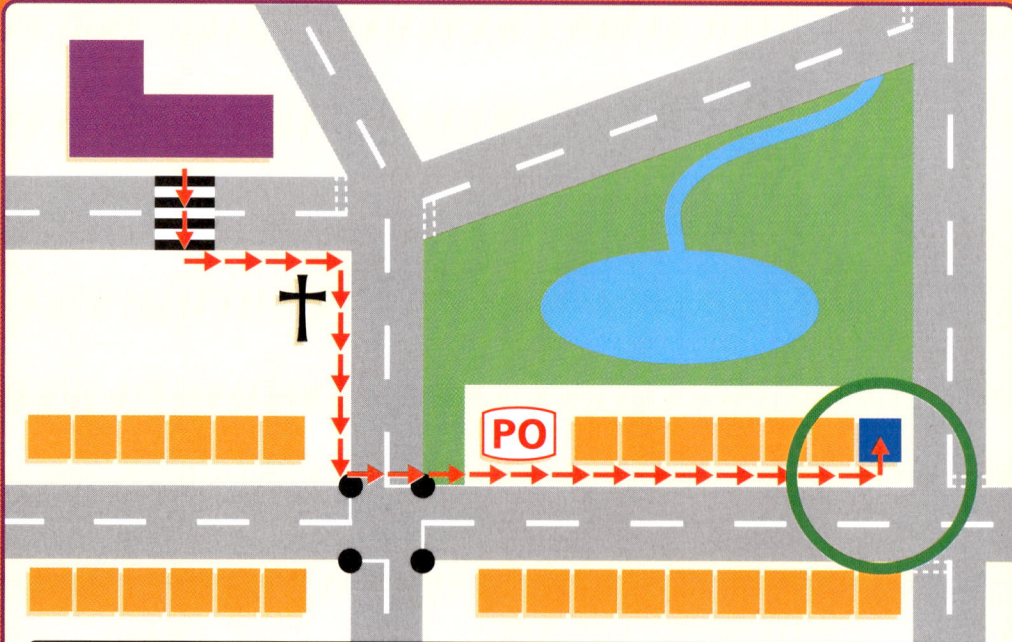

Key

School		PO	Post office
Zebra crossing			House
Church			My House
Traffic lights			Grass
			Pond

PO

18

14

19

Welcome to my party!

20

PARTY!

21

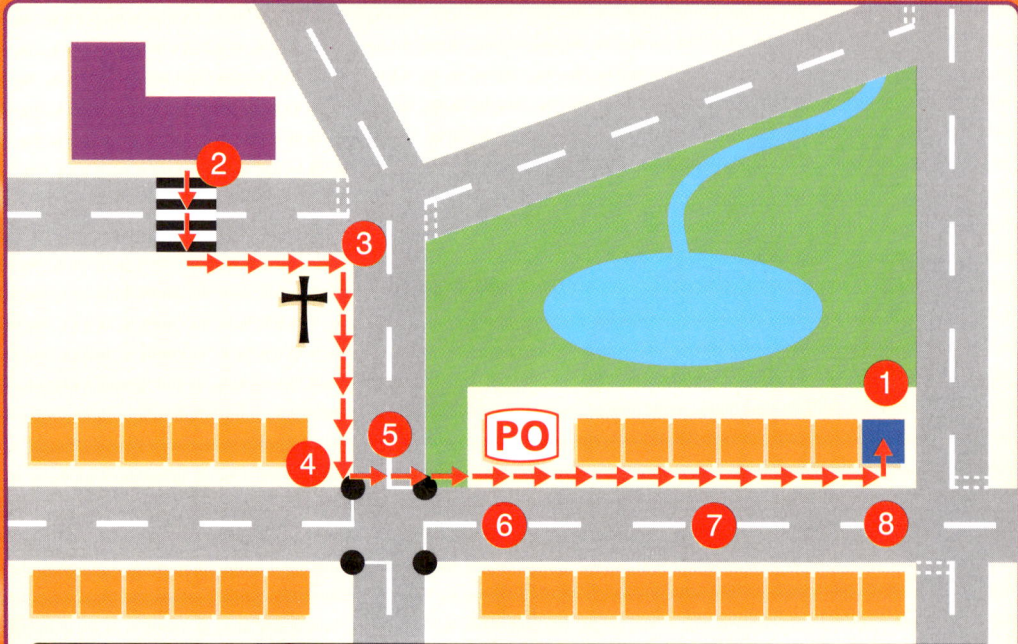

My route

Key

School	PO	Post office
Zebra crossing		House
Church		My House
		Grass
Traffic lights		Pond

22

1. Find my house on the map.

2. First cross at the zebra crossing.

3. Turn right past the church.

4. Then carry on until you get to the traffic lights.

5. Now turn left and when the green man is showing, cross the road.

6. Walk past the park and look out for the post office.

7. Count six houses past the post office.

8. Look for the blue door with the balloons on it.

Index

A a
B b
C c
D d
E e
F f
G g
H h
I i
J j
K k
L l
M m
N n
O o
P p
Q q
R r
S s
T t
U u
V v
W w
X x
Y y
Z z